How? What? Why?

How long did I sleep?

Jim Pipe

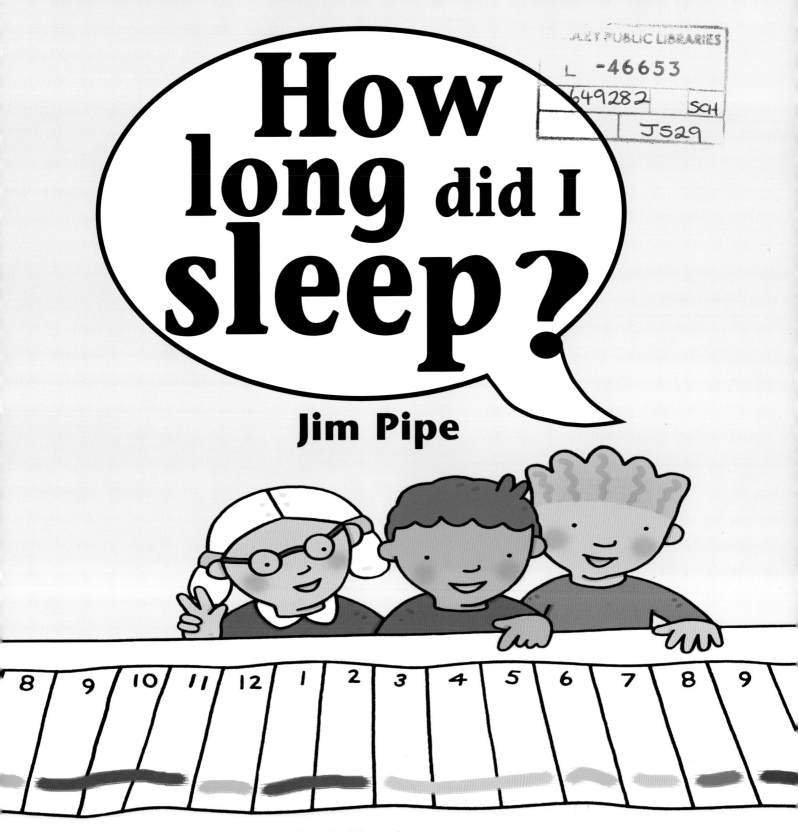

Aladdin/Watts
London • Sydney

How long does Steve sleep?

It is time to go home. Jo, Steve, Amy and Zack are coming out of school. Steve's mum is waiting to pick them up, and asks about their day.

Today has whizzed by. We got to school at 9 o'clock, and now it's after 3!

There's still lots of time for you to play before dinner.

2

Let's see how the children find out.

Let's make a 24-hour chart of your day, Steve.

1

I get up at 7 a.m. Then I wash, dress and eat breakfast.

From 9 to 3 I'm at school. I have lunch for an hour at 12.

2

I play at home from 3 to 6, when I have dinner. I play for another hour, then I get ready for bed.

4

You spend 5 hours at school, 5 hours eating or getting ready and 4 hours playing.

3

You spend more time asleep than doing anything else: 10 hours!

Why it works

Clocks tell us what time it is. They also tell us how long we take to do things. Steve used clocks at home and at school to work out how he spent his day. Some clocks also tell us if it is before midday, a.m., or after midday, p.m. See if you can make a chart of your own day!

Solve the puzzle!

Are you good at guessing the time? Check the time, then draw a picture of a clock. Guess how long it took, then check the time again (see page 22).

How long do leaves take to grow?

The children are looking at the plants in the greenhouse. They decide to grow their own plants in jars, but they are not sure how long it will take.

Let's time how long it takes for beans to grow leaves.

We can time them using that clock.

Let's see how the children find out.

It's Tuesday the 26th. Leaves and roots are just starting to show.

3

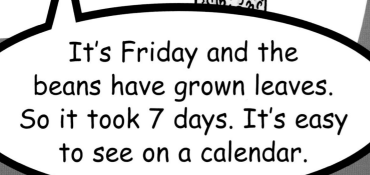

4

It's Friday and the beans have grown leaves. So it took 7 days. It's easy to see on a calendar.

Why it works

Some things happen fast, others happen slowly. So we use different units, or lengths, of time. If we want to know the time in hours, minutes or seconds, we use a clock or a watch. When we think about things that will happen next week, or next month, we use a calendar. A calendar divides each year into the twelve months and shows the seven days of the week.

Solve the puzzle

What units of time would you use to time a short race, to bake a cake or to say your age?

9

How can the sun tell us the time?

The children are playing out in the garden on a sunny day. Amy gets too hot and decides to sit in the shadow of a tree.

Don't fall asleep, Amy. The tree's shadow will move and the sun might burn you.

Why does the shadow move?

10

11

Let's see how the children find out.

Why it works

As the sun's position changes in the sky, the shadows it makes on the ground move as well. You can tell the time if you mark a stick's moving shadow with stones. In the past, people used sundials to tell the time. A triangle shape in the middle of a sundial makes a shadow (see page 11), and marks around the edge show the hour as the shadow moves. But you can't use it at night!

Solve the puzzle

Can you tell the time by where the sun is? Think about where the sun rises and sets.

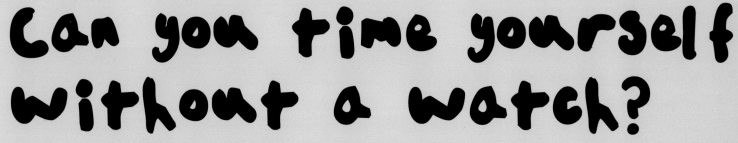

Can you time yourself without a watch?

Amy wants to time how many skips each person can do in a minute. But she can't remember where her watch is!

How can we time ourselves? Perhaps we could count up to 20 out loud.

It's hard to count at the same speed every time.

Let's see how the children find out.

3

When all the sand has run into the jar, the time is up.

It always takes the same time. So we can measure time without a watch.

Why it works

If you always use exactly the same amount of sand, it always takes the same time to trickle down into the jar. Using the sand clock, Amy could see how many skips Jo can do before all the sand runs out. Then she could use it again to time Steve and Zack.

Solve the puzzle

Can you make a water clock? Ask an adult to make a tiny hole in a paper cup. Then put it over a jar and see how long exactly one cup of water takes to trickle through the hole.

17

Why does a pendulum swing?

The children visit Steve's grandfather. He has an old clock in his house. Inside the clock case, a long pendulum swings from side to side.

Why does a pendulum swing?

Dad said the swinging weight keeps the clock in time.

19

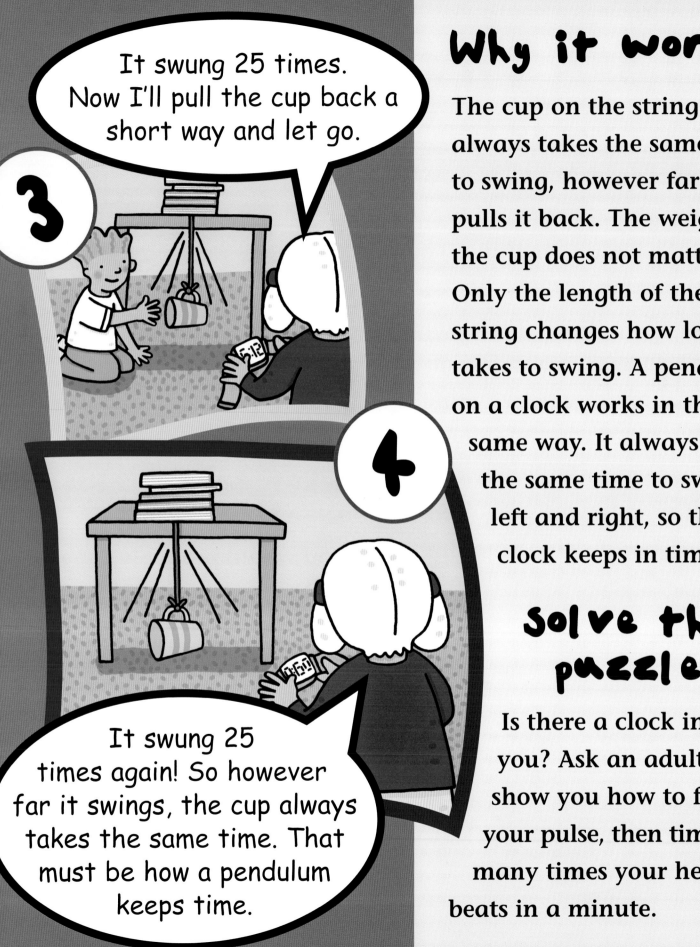

Why it works

The cup on the string always takes the same time to swing, however far Zack pulls it back. The weight of the cup does not matter. Only the length of the string changes how long it takes to swing. A pendulum on a clock works in the same way. It always takes the same time to swing left and right, so the clock keeps in time.

Solve the puzzle

Is there a clock inside you? Ask an adult to show you how to feel your pulse, then time how many times your heart beats in a minute.

Did you solve the puzzles?

Are you good at guessing the time?

People often guess how long it will take to do something. They say things like, "I'll be back in 5 minutes" or "It will take half an hour". To make your own guess, think of another activity that usually takes you the same time. Perhaps you usually spend about 10 minutes having a shower, or half an hour eating your dinner.

What unit of time would you use?

You would probably time a short race in seconds because it happens quickly. You might use minutes or hours to time how long it takes to bake a cake, and years to describe how old you are. Can you think of other activities that might take you days, weeks or months?

Can you tell the time by where the sun is?

Yes, looking at shadows can help you guess the time (but NEVER look straight at the sun). In the morning, the sun rises in the sky and shadows get shorter. After midday, the sun gets lower, and shadows get longer again.

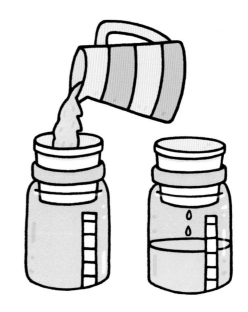

Is there a clock inside you?

If you measure your pulse when you are sitting still, you should feel your heart beat about 90-100 times a minute. What happens if you run around for five minutes then time it again?

Can you make a water clock?

A water clock works like the sand clock on page 17. The water should always take the same time to trickle into the jar. If you stick a piece of paper on the side with lines 1 centimetre apart you can time different activities.

23

Index

© Aladdin Books Ltd 2003

Designed and produced by
Aladdin Books Ltd
28 Percy Street
London W1T 2BZ

First published in
Great Britain in 2003 by
Franklin Watts
96 Leonard Street
London EC2A 4XD

ISBN 0 7496 4972 0

A catalogue record for this book is
available from the British Library.

Printed in U.A.E.
All rights reserved

Literacy Consultant
Jackie Holderness
Westminster Institute of Education
Oxford Brookes University

Science Consultants
Helen Wilson and David Coates
Westminster Institute of Education
Oxford Brookes University

Science Tester
Alex Laar

Design
Flick, Book Design and Graphics

Illustration
Jo Moore